Here Lies Price

ff

HERE
LIES PRICE

Susan Price

faber and faber
LONDON · BOSTON

First published in 1987
by Faber and Faber Limited
3 Queen Square, London, WC1N 3AU

Photoset by Parker Typesetting Service, Leicester
Printed in Great Britain by
Redwood Burn Ltd, Trowbridge, Wiltshire

British Library Cataloguing in Publication Data

Price, Susan
Here lies price: tall tales and ghost stories
I. Title
823'.914[J]   PZ7

ISBN 0-571-14804-2

Contents

The Kettle

Here's a true story about liars.

There were once three colliers named Rainbow, Linnet and Tip-Tap. Rainbow was called Rainbow because his legs were each as bowed as a rainbow; and Linnet was called Linnet because he sang like a seven-coloured linnet. I'm not sure why Tip-Tap was called Tip-Tap, but home-brewed beer is called tip-tap sometimes.

Anyway, the three of them were on their way home from work when they came on a kettle lying in the road. It had fallen off a cart and it was lying there, lost – and it was a good kettle, a big one. So all three of them wanted it – Rainbow for his wife, Tip-Tap for himself, and Linnet for his mother.

Tip-Tap said, 'We won't fall out. We'll have a contest to decide. The one of us that tells the biggest lie wins the kettle.'

Since they were passing the church, they went into the churchyard to hold the contest. Tip-Tap put the kettle on top of a gravestone, and they tossed a coin to see who would start.

It was Linnet. 'When I went to the Oldbury Wake,' he said, 'I did see some sights. I saw a woman that swallowed herself; I saw a blue bottle fly, and I watched a man carry hisself up a ladder

1

in two buckets.'

Rainbow won the next toss. 'I went to the Wake with me old father,' he said. 'The old man got drunk! He had a go on one of them stalls where you throw a ball to knock a skittle down, and he was so drunk he was a public danger. The showman gave him a tortoise for a prize, to get rid of him. Half an hour later me Dad comes back, he says to the showman, "Have you got any more of them crusty meat pies?" '

'My turn,' Tip-Tap said. 'Do you remember that dog I used to have; the bull-terrier? Beautiful dog. He could talk, you know. He could. Chaps in the pub wouldn't believe me. They bet me ten shillings he couldn't. Well, I knew he could. So I says to Bull, "Speak to the masters, Bull; show 'em you can talk!" Bull never says a word. He just looks up at me and thumps his tail. "Talk, Bull," I says. I begged him. But he wouldn't. So I had to pay up, and I went off home as wicked as a wasp. Bull comes running after me. "Don't come wagging your tail after me," I says. "I'll kick you in the cut as soon as look at you. You cost me ten shillings tonight." And Bull says, "I did. But think how much you'll win next time!" '

Just then the Vicar came out of the church and saw three dirty colliers sitting on the gravestones in his churchyard, all laughing out loud in the most common manner.

The Vicar went over to them, smiling and smiling, and said, 'Well, lads, and what are you up to?'

'Never mind we, Gaffer,' Tip-Tap said. 'We'm

just seeing who can tell the biggest lie.'

The Vicar was shocked. 'Really, boys; in a churchyard? To tell lies is a sin, you know. God doesn't like it. We must never, never tell lies.'

'Don't you ever tell lies, Master?' Linnet asked.

'No, young man, I never do, and I'll tell you why. When I was just a little boy, my mother took me on her lap and she said, 'Now, Alfred, promise me that you'll never, never tell an untruth as long as you live.' And I promised, and, do you know, boys, I have never broken that promise.'

Tip-Tap got up, took the kettle from the gravestone, and put it into the Vicar's hands.

'Vicar,' Tip-Tap said, 'you've won that kettle fair and square. I never heard such a whopper in me life.'

And the Vicar stood there, with the kettle in his hands, while Linnet, Rainbow and Tip-Tap went out through the church gate.

Well, easy come, easy go. It was worth losing the kettle.

My Great-Grandfather's Grave-Digging

This is a true story because it happened to my great-grandfather.

His name was Jody Price, and he was a coal miner until his cough got so bad that he was sacked. He had chronic bronchitis and used to cough himself unconscious, and you can't cut coal when you're unconscious. So he was no use and was turned off.

All that coughing had given him a deep, wheezing, groaning voice that sounded as if it was coming from a mile deep, from the coal at the bottom of the pits. You could always tell when Jody was coming because he soon got out of breath, and then you could hear him panting and wheezing yards away.

After he left the pit he got a job as a gravedigger. He would dig a grave the day before it was needed, get his pay from the verger, and then wander into the Wander Inn. He'd have a couple of halves in there, and then he'd drop in at the Dew Drop Inn and have another couple. He'd play a game of dominoes, have a chat, and then go wheezing home.

He always took a short cut home through the graveyard, and one dark night he fell into the grave

4

he'd dug that afternoon. He lay on his back at the bottom, looking at his feet waving over his head and wondering how they'd got there, until he realized what had happened.

It wasn't easy getting out because the grave was six feet deep, and Jody was only five feet tall – and he was drunk, and the sides of the grave were soft and muddy. He kept slithering back to the bottom, plastered in mud. If he'd had his shovel he could have stood on that, but it was up on top, stuck in the pile of dirt that he'd dug out to make the grave. He got tired and breathless, and made up his mind to sit in the grave all night, until somebody came along to give him a hand out in the morning.

So he hunched himself in a corner of the grave, hugged his hands under his armpits, and tried to forget about the mud and the cold wet. He dozed, but nearly had the life frightened out of him by a sudden rush, thump and a yell. He peered about in the dark. There was a lot of cussing and muttering going on close by, and something was blundering about, thumping into the sides of the grave. Somebody else had come tipsy through the grave-yard and had tumbled in.

Jody didn't say anything to let this other man know he was there. How was Jody to know who it was, in the dark? The kind of people who fall into graves at that time of night aren't always the kind of people you want to know.

The stranger kept leaping at the sides of the grave, and falling back with a thud and lumps of

5

mud. Soon he was gasping for breath, but he was no nearer getting out. Jody always did a good job and any grave of his was a good six feet deep, and a few inches over. Jody knew the stranger was never going to get out, if he tried all night. So, in the end, he felt sorry for the man, and he spoke up from his dark corner, in his deep, groaning, wheezing voice. He said:

'You won't get out of my grave. I been trying for ages, and I can't.'

But before Jody had finished speaking, that other man was out of the grave and halfway across the churchyard.

'He could jump like that,' Great-Grandad said, 'and yet he never turned back to give me hand. He never even said goodnight. Ain't there some camels in this world?'

The Troll Sister

I know that this must be a true story, because I read it in a book.

The book said it happened in Iceland, in the days when the people used to go into the mountains every year, to gather tall basketfuls of a moss which grew up there. It was a food and a medicine.

The people used to set up tents in the mountain meadows, and camp there until they'd gathered enough moss to last them for a year; and, one year, there were three sisters sharing a tent. Their names were Thora, Unn, and Gerda.

All three of them worked hard all day, walking, bending, pulling the moss and filling their baskets. At night they slept deeply, worn out – and so it was strange for the youngest sister, Gerda, to wake in the middle of the night. Her head ached and her eyes burned with sleepiness, and she would have gone straight back to sleep if she hadn't felt cold. She soon found out that she was cold because Thora, the eldest of them, was gone from beside her. Gerda reached out to Unn and shook her awake. That took time, and more time to explain what was the matter when Unn awoke. But then they both poked their heads from the tent, to see if their sister was out there.

7

The moon and stars were shining whitely, and the air was clear. They could see for a long way. Thora was walking over the little meadow towards the further rise of mountains. She was walking in a strange way – a stomping step, then a halt, then another heavy step. Even so, she was moving quickly, and she took no notice when they shouted to her, even though they screamed until their throats hurt and woke the people in other tents.

Then Gerda saw something, and pointed. On an outcrop of stone, a little cliff, on the mountainside, stood a troll.

The troll was stretching out its long arms towards their sister, and then crossing its arms over its chest. Every time it did this, Thora took another step. The troll was calling her away.

Unn and Gerda did more than shout then. They both crawled out of their tent and began running after their eldest sister, in their underskirts. But there were many black shadows, at which they must stop, in case they were holes; and stones that bruised their feet, and hillocks they tripped over – while Thora went steadily on as the troll summoned her with its slow, grand movements. They saw Thora reach the mountainside and climb to the troll; and they saw her go away with it; and there was nothing they could do.

The next day all the men and women who had gathered to pick moss searched the mountains for the missing girl, but they didn't find her. Every night one of her sisters sat awake by a fire, hoping she might come back, but she didn't. When it was time to go home, some of the people stayed behind, hoping that now the girl would come back. It was hard to know when to give up waiting. It always seemed worth staying one more day. But when it was certainly autumn, even Unn and Gerda had to leave the mountains.

They missed their sister, and often talked about her, saying that perhaps she would come walking in at the door one day – or maybe, when they went moss-picking the next year, she would turn up. But both of them really believed that Thora was dead. The troll would have eaten her. Or, even if the troll had not . . . What was she living on, up there, in the wild mountains, with the trolls? Those who eat a troll's food become trolls themselves.

The next year, when it was moss-gathering time again, the sisters were careful to go back to the same meadow, and to set up their tent in the same spot. And one day, as they were stooping to rip up the moss, Unn straightened and saw Thora, their lost sister, standing in front of them. She hit Gerda on the shoulder, and she straightened too, and she saw.

Thora was standing at a distance from them, standing quietly and watching them. She had made no noise as she had come near. They could tell it was Thora, but she had changed. Her skin had been roughened and darkened by the cold, wind and wet she had suffered. Her long hair was greyer than it had been, and tangled. Her face

9

seemed broader, stupider than they remembered.

'Thora!' her sisters cried out, and started forward, but stopped at once, for their sister gave no sign of understanding, or of welcoming them. The way she stood there, so solid, and stared, frightened them.

'Don't you remember us, Thora?' Gerda asked.

Their strange sister stared silently a long time before saying, as if her voice was hard to use, 'Gerda.'

'And where do you live, Thora?' asked Unn.

'I lived –' Thora said slowly, and reached her hands towards them. Her face had something like sadness in it. 'No more,' she said.

Unn thought that if she could turn Thora's thoughts towards God and the Virgin she might be saved from the trolls, and so said, 'What do you believe in, Thora?'

There was another long, long silence between them, in the meadow, before Thora said, with difficulty, 'I believe in . . . Jesus. And the Saints.'

'Come home with us!' Gerda said, and both girls started forward to catch their sister's hands – but Thora turned her back on them and, with long, fast strides, went away into the mountains; and they couldn't catch her.

On other days Thora returned, to silently watch the people at work. If anyone tried to approach her, she hurried away. She would listen to the pleas of her sisters from a little distance, but would not let them come near her; and when they went home, she stayed in the mountains with the trolls.

A whole year later, Thora appeared again, on the first day of the moss-gathering, and stood before her sisters. They were silent, afraid to speak to her. Now her shoulders were thick and hunched like a troll's shoulders. Her hair was as grey, harsh and coarse as a mess of unravelled rope. Her face was so thickened and altered that it was only by the look of her eyes that they recognized her.

'What is your name?' Gerda asked eventually; and they went on asking all day; but not once did they hear any answer.

When they saw her again, they asked her, 'Where do you live?' But this troll-sister of theirs looked at them silently from her ugly, fierce troll-face, and answered nothing, though the tears ran down their faces for her.

The third time they saw her they asked, with little hope of any reply, 'What do you believe in?'

'Jesus!' said the troll suddenly; and then turned and made for the mountains with long troll-strides.

'If she still remembers even that much of our life together, there is still hope she might return to us,' said Unn. But their lost sister came to watch them no more that season, as if remembering Jesus had alarmed her.

The third year they went again to the mountains, but their lost sister did not appear on the first day, or the second, and they had little hope of her coming at all. But on the very last day of their stay, she did come, and stood and stared at them. They could hardly bear to look back at her because she was exactly like a troll.

They asked her what was her name, and where did she live, and got no answer but a stolid, frowning stare.

'What do you believe in?' they asked her, and she raised her head, and stopped frowning, as if she knew those words.

'What do you believe in?' Gerda cried.

The troll-sister's mouth gaped; she made a noise.

'What do you believe in?' shouted Unn.

And the troll-sister said, 'Trunt, Trunt, and the Trolls in the Fells.'

Then she turned and walked away, and, since then, has been seen by no one – or, if she has, they could not tell her from any other troll.

And what she meant by her last words, no one knows – or cares to find out.

Lost Vanya

This may be true or it may not; but the person who told it me said it was true.

There were once two cousins named Vanya and Misha. They had been brought up together, and had always been closer than brothers. When people saw Vanya, then they looked round for Misha; when they met Misha, they called out a greeting to Vanya, knowing he couldn't be far away.

Vanya's and Misha's favourite game was boasting to each other of what they would do when they were grown men. In bed, before they fell asleep; in fields, lying idle; at the dinner-table, when they should have been eating, they would whisper together.

'I shall build my own house, and keep my own cattle, and be a big man in the village,' Misha said.

'Your house won't be as big as mine,' Vanya would answer, 'and you won't have as many cattle. And I shall breed horses too.'

Then they would giggle and punch each other, and try to think of other ways to outdo each other.

'I shall travel far away – to Africa, to England, to Spain!' said Misha. 'I shall come back with things no one has ever seen! And everyone will want to buy them, and I shall be rich and build a palace!'

'I shall go further and bring back more and be richer and build two palaces!' said Vanya.

They grew to be young men, but they were still friends and they still played the boasting-game. 'I shall marry the most beautiful girl in the world,' said Misha. 'Other men will faint to see her. I shall marry her, and we shall have fifty children and be the happiest family on earth!'

'I shall marry a girl twice as beautiful, and have a hundred and fifty children!' said Vanya. 'I'm bound to be happy, because in that crowd I shall never be lonely.'

But before Misha was nineteen, he died, of consumption. As Misha lay in his coffin, Vanya tucked a full bottle of vodka in beside him, to help his friend keep away the cold of the earth. They buried Misha beneath a birch-tree in the graveyard, and it was a long, long time before people stopped expecting to see him at Vanya's side. It was even longer before Vanya stopped looking for him there.

But all things pass; and Vanya went on growing older. In his twenty-second year, he asked Elenia to marry him, and she said yes. No one fainted at the sight of her, but she was very pretty, and Vanya was as happy as he could have been if his old boast had come true.

On the day of the wedding, they set off in carts decorated with flowers, and everyone was happy until they passed the graveyard. There Vanya saw the birch-tree beneath which Misha lay buried. He

14

remembered their game, and realized that here he was, on his wedding day, making his boast good, in part, at least; while poor Misha had been cold and buried for years, with no hope of matching him. He had far surpassed Misha, just as he had always sworn he would do, but had never believed that he could. Vanya felt that he should apologize to Misha because he was alive and Misha was dead. So he stopped the cart, climbed down, and walked alone into the graveyard.

His bride, and their two families, and all the guests, watched him from the road, and called to him to hurry. He waved and said that he only wanted a minute, just a minute . . .

Looking down at the grave, feeling foolish, feeling tears behind his eyes, he muttered, 'Misha . . . can you hear me? Here I am – Vanya – you remember – and it's my wedding day! So I've come to tell you that, Misha . . . and to wish you well . . . wherever you are . . .'

The ground at his feet gave a quiver, and the grave opened. There lay Misha, in his coffin, looking just as he had when they'd buried him, except that he was whiter. And more gaunt. He raised an arm towards Vanya, and in his hand there was a bottle of vodka.

'Vanya, my friend, bless you! You remember me, though I've been dead so long, even on your wedding day you remember me! You would make me cry, Vanushka, if I could cry. And here is the vodka you gave me – I owe you so much! Please, Vanya,

15

little brother, come and drink a glass of vodka with me on your wedding day.'

'But, Misha – you're dead!'

'Does that matter? Do you fear me now, because I'm dead? Oh, Vanushka; did I ever give you any reason to fear me?' And Misha held out his blue-white, bone hand for Vanya to take. 'Don't deny me this moment of friendship,' the dead man pleaded. 'I always believed I would drink a toast to you on your wedding day. Stay a few moments, Vanushka; long enough to drink a glass and speak a word or two.'

How could Vanya refuse? 'Just a minute, then,' he said, and took Misha's hand.

The grip of the dead hand was hard and cold. With a strong pull, Misha drew Vanya forward into the grave, as if he drew him over the threshold of a house – while Misha himself retreated further in. The wedding-guests, watching from the road, raised a cry of distress as they saw Vanya step into the earth.

All light vanished from Vanya's sight as the grave closed; but then a blue light, like the blue flames of corpse-candles, lit Misha's death-head.

Vanya said, 'When I put that bottle in your coffin, I never expected to share it!' They were crammed together in the narrow space – the grave is a small house. The cold moisture of the earth soaked through Vanya's clothes, and violet worms wriggled from the walls in the blue light.

'To you and your wife on your wedding day!'

said Misha. 'May you have a long and happy life together, and a houseful of children!' He drank from the bottle, and passed it to Vanya.

Vanya would have liked to wipe the neck of the bottle, but he didn't want to hurt his friend's feelings. 'To me,' he said, and bravely drank before passing the bottle back.

'Who is your wife? Did I know her?' Misha asked. The walls of damp earth soaked up his voice, and the sound was like mice whispering in a nest.

'Yes; she is Elenia Gregorovna. And now, Misha, I must – '

'Ah! A beautiful girl – even when I knew her, you could see she would be a beauty! Congratulations, Vanushka! A toast to Elenia Gregorovna! Long life and good health to her, a child every year to her!' And he drank, and handed the bottle to Vanya.

'I'll gladly drink to that,' Vanya said, 'but then I must go, Misha. They are waiting for me, you know, and I said I would only stay – '

'Drink, drink!' said Misha.

'I will, but . . . You will open the door and let me out, won't you, Misha?'

'Vanya! Do you think I will keep you here? I – your friend?'

'No, of course you wouldn't!' Vanya said, and laughed, and drank to his bride. 'Here's your bottle, Misha – good of you to keep it until I came! Now do your trick and open the door – '

17

'One more drink,' Misha said.

'Oh no, Misha . . . You must understand how nervous I am, sitting here in a grave; you understand, Misha. It's not the same as in the old days. And my bride will think I've deserted her. I'd love to stay and chat, but really I can't –'

'Just one drink to me,' said the dead man. 'Won't you, on your wedding day, spare just a moment to drink a toast to me?'

Vanya took the bottle and said, 'Here's to my friend, Misha, my friend still, though he's dead. May he lie at peace in his grave . . . Is that good?'

'Very good,' Misha said. 'Thank you, Vanushka. You make me happy.' And he watched with pleasure as Vanya drank to him and, taking the bottle back, he drank too. 'Now, I suppose you must go,' he said sadly. 'Goodbye, Vanya. I shall never see you again.'

Vanya felt tears come to his eyes. 'In Heaven, surely?'

'No,' said Misha, still more sadly. He leaned forward and hugged Vanya, smelling strongly of earth. He kissed Vanya's cheeks with cold lips. 'Goodbye, goodbye,' he said, so sadly that Vanya almost cried.

Daylight lit the grave, and Vanya knew that the grave had opened. Sad for his friend, but still relieved to be escaping into the clear air, he clambered from the grave, calling goodbye. Before he could blink, the grave had closed again, and was as it had been before; as if it had never opened.

Vanya straightened and stretched and turned to the road where his wedding party was waiting – and the road was quite empty; no people, no carts, no horses.

He must have been longer than he'd thought, and they'd gone on without him. He ran from the graveyard to the church – but the church was deserted too. No one was near it.

'They think I've run away,' he thought, in a panic. 'Elenia will be angry with me.' And he ran from the church to the village. At least the running warmed him. He was so cold after being in the grave that he couldn't feel the sun.

'Has the wedding party come this way?' he shouted to a man in a field.

'What wedding party?' the man asked. 'Who are you?'

'Who are you?' Vanya asked, for the man was a stranger. They stood staring at each other.

'Who marries at this time of year?' said the man.

'It's summer!' Vanya exclaimed. The end of summer, when the harvest was in – the best time of all for marrying and feasting!

'Summer!' said the man, and sounded so surprised that Vanya looked around and saw – how could he not have noticed? – that it was not summer. The fields were bare and hard; the sky over them was grey. Only the pine trees had leaves. The chill of the grave had followed him out of the earth.

'Misha, what have you done to me?'

He walked along the hard road to his village –

but it was not his village any more. There was not a face that he knew. Houses that had been new that morning were now old, and there were houses that he had never seen. He knocked at doors, and the people looked at him as if he was a stranger. He asked for Elenia Gregorovna, and was taken to her, but it was a middle-aged woman, not his Elenia.

'Misha, Misha, why did you do this?' he said. The people asked him what he meant, and when he tried to explain, they became afraid and drew away from him.

'It's him, it's Lost Vanya!' said the middle-aged Elenia. 'My great-grandmother,' she said, leaning towards Vanya, 'was named Elenia Gregorovna and when she was a young girl she went to be married to a man named Vanya. But at the church-yard he got down to visit the grave of a dead friend . . . he vanished in front of their eyes, and never came back. Are you him? Are you Lost Vanya?'

But Vanya turned away from her, saying, 'Misha, why have you done this to me?' The people followed him, and saw him leave the village and walk the road to the churchyard. Poor wanderer; homeless, graveless.

He went into the churchyard and to an old birch-tree. Under it was a forgotten grave, so old that no one remembered who was buried there, or cared for it. 'Misha – ?' said Lost Vanya, and then, as his foot touched the grave, he crumbled away, and was truly lost.

The Haunted Inn

This story is so true, you'll be told it in a dozen pubs. But I was told it in a pub called The Struggling Man.

A salesman came in one night, I was told, and said, 'Can you put me up?'

Before the landlord could say yes or no, one of the regulars leaned over and said, 'How about giving him the haunted room?'

The salesman, after a hard day's selling, was only in the mood for sleep. He said, 'This isn't another pub with a haunted room, is it?'

'What do you mean?' the landlord asked.

'Every pub I've stayed in had a haunted room,' said the salesman. 'I wish the breweries would think up a new advertising stunt. I'm sick of that one.'

The landlord was hurt. 'I beg your pardon, but my pub really is haunted.'

'What by?' asked the salesman. 'A grey lady? A green lady? A yellow-come-purple-with-orange-spots-lady? It always is a lady of one colour or another.'

'I've never seen it, so I don't know what it is,' said the landlord. 'And I don't want to see it neither, because I do know that whenever anybody's slept in that room, they've been raving screaming mad the next morning. That's why I never let anybody sleep in there.'

'Who told you all that?' the salesman asked.

'Well . . . The man who was landlord here before me.'

'And had *he* ever seen it?'

'Well, I don't know . . .'

"Course he hadn't,' said the salesman.

'You wouldn't catch me sleeping in that room, anyway,' said the regular.

'I would,' said the salesman. 'You want a bet?'

'Don't start that,' said the landlord. 'I've never let anybody sleep in there, and I'm not about to.'

But the regular said to the salesman. 'Will you still be here tomorrow night? I'll buy you a double if you sleep in that room tonight – with the door locked on the outside.'

'If I can search the room before the door's locked, you're on,' said the salesman. 'But I'm not so much green as cabbage-looking. You won't catch me out with tape-recordings of groans hidden in the wardrobe.'

'We won't need to bother with that kind of mal-arky if you're locked in the haunted room,' said the regular.

'Now I'm sorry to disappoint you gents,' said the landlord, 'but nobody is going to sleep in that room tonight or any other night.'

Everyone disagreed. The regular customers wanted the fun of the bet, and they wanted to see

22

the salesman brought down a peg or two – and the salesman wanted to prove that there was no ghost and bring the locals down a peg or three. All of them badgered the landlord to let the haunted room to the salesman.

The landlord gave way. After all, it was the salesman's business if he wanted to sleep with a ghost, and maybe it was stupid to worry about ghosts in this day and age.

The landlord found the key of the haunted room and led the way upstairs. A lot of customers from the bar followed, as well as the salesman with his luggage. It was quite a crush.

The haunted room was at the back of the pub, at the end of a long and badly-lit corridor that smelt of dust and paint. By the time they reached it, they couldn't hear a sound from the bar, and even the people who'd followed them upstairs had gone quiet. The landlord opened the door and the salesman went in.

'A four-poster bed!' he cried, dropping his suitcase.

'Good, isn't it?' said the landlord. 'It's a hundred years old, you know.' He went over and drew the curtains.

'A four-poster bed in the haunted room!' said the salesman. 'You put it in here on purpose, to make the place look spookier!'

'I bet there's a good many died in that bed,' said the regular. 'Sleep tight!' Everybody laughed.

'All out into the hall, while I search,' said the

salesman, and shooed them out of the room. 'If there's a ghost, watch me find it!'

The regulars and the landlord stood on the landing and watched the salesman make a complete search of every possible hiding-place in the haunted room. He looked in the bed and under it; up the chimney; in the cupboards and the cupboard drawers; behind the curtains at the window, behind the door. He didn't find anything.

'OK, mugs,' he said. 'You can lock me in. I'll see you tomorrow night, and you can have a double whisky waiting for me.'

'Last chance to change your mind,' said the landlord.

The salesman said, 'Get away!' So the landlord locked the door from the outside, and took the key with him. He and his customers all went laughing down the corridor, back to the bar for some after-hours drinking. Once they'd gone, that part of the house was silent.

But the salesman was a man who really didn't believe in ghosts. He undressed and hung his clothes on hangers, brushing them carefully. He peeled off his wig and put it on his bedside table. He put on his pyjamas, put off the light and, in the dark, found his way to the four-poster bed.

A soft curtain brushed his face. The old bed creaked as he knelt on it and, as he rolled back the covers a warm, comfortable smell of clean sheets and blankets rose up. He lay on his side and covered himself, ready for sleep. Then, 'I'm glad we're locked in for the night,' said a voice at his ear.

In the morning, even the salesman's wig had turned white.

I wonder why the pub was called The Struggling Man?

The Devil and the P.M.

This is a story that I think must be true.

One morning, out walking, the Prime Minister met with the Devil, who lifted his hat politely, swung his tail over his arm and called out, "Morning!" This gave the Prime Minister quite a turn.

'I have a vacancy in Hell,' said the Devil, eyeing the P.M. as he spoke. 'It's a choice situation – particularly hot, with a full complement of imps and shrikes to provide the tortures. I don't want to waste it. So I've come to Earth to find exactly the right person for it.'

The door of a house they were passing opened, and a man came out in a hurry. Behind him came his wife, and the wife yelled, 'Go on, go on, run away! Don't listen to me! I wish I'd never laid eyes on you!'

The P.M. pointed to the man. 'There's a likely sort. Take that man over there, Your Satanic Majesty.'

'He would never do at all,' said the Devil. 'What has he ever done, and who wishes him in Hell? I can't touch anyone who hasn't been wished into my power.'

A small boy came dashing out of the house, elbowing past his angry mother. 'You little nuisance, you horror, you good-for-nothing!' she yelled. 'Come back here and I'll give you something to wear! Oh, I wish the Devil'd have away with you!'

'There you are, Your Majesty,' said the Prime Minister helpfully. 'That boy has such criminal tendencies that even his mother wishes him with you in Hell. Take him – he'll fill your vacancy!'

But the Devil only smiled and shook his head. 'Oh no,' he said. 'With her lips she wishes him in my power, but if truth be told, she'd fight me to Hell and back if I looked at him. No, no; the wish must be made with more than the lips if it's to give a soul to me.'

As they were speaking a dog ran out of the house after the boy. It nearly knocked the mother off her feet. 'Oh damn that dog!' she cried. 'Damn that dog into Hell – let the Devil have it. I'm sick of it!'

'That was meant!' said the Prime Minister. 'Take the dog, Your Majesty – they shouldn't be keeping it anyway – Quickly! Before it's too far away!'

The Devil laughed. 'Nothing is ever out of my reach, but that dog was never in my power. The woman no more means what she said about the dog than what she said about the boy. Her curses are air.'

Then the woman caught sight of the P.M. 'Oh!' she cried. 'There's that Prime Minister! If anybody deserves to be in Hell, it's that one. May the Devil take you, you pestilence! May you get what you deserve! May it be done unto you as you've done unto others!'

Then the P.M. felt the Devil's claws. 'Oh, that was meant, that came from the heart!' said the Devil. 'In her heart, in her blood, in the very bones of her, she wishes you a position in my company!'

And there had to be a reshuffle and a by-election.

The Curse on the Willow

This is a story about Jesus, so it must be true. It's a story about when He was a little boy, before He cared much about being the son of God.

Jesus was the son of Mary and God, but God was up in Heaven and couldn't be with them, so instead they lived with Joseph, a poor carpenter, in the village of Bethlehem. Mary kept house for Joseph, and while she was working she would send Jesus out into the street to play. There wasn't much traffic to worry about then – only donkeys and horses. And Jesus would play tag, and ball, and hide-and-seek, and all the other games with the other children.

Now, in Bethlehem, there were three rich men – you always find a few rich men where there are a lot of poor ones. These three rich men all had wives, and they all had sons; and these three rich little boys were always dressed in the most beautiful clothes, and always had the most expensive toys to play with. They played together, just the three of them, because their rich mothers and their rich fathers didn't want them to play with the poor children.

One day these three rich little boys came out to play with marbles, beautiful marbles, glowing blue, green and amber, with swirls of different colours inside them. All the poor children went up to look at them, and they all wanted to play with them, but the rich boys told them to go away.

Jesus wanted to play with the marbles too, and He went up to the rich boys and asked them, straight, if He could play.

'We're not going to let *you* touch our marbles,' said the first rich boy. 'You're too dirty and poor. You'd spoil them.'

'You're just the carpenter's son,' said the second. 'Your father has dirty hands. My mother says I'm not to have anything to do with You.'

'My mother says that too,' said the third rich boy. 'She says Your mother has to do all her own work, so Your mother has dirty hands too, all greasy and dirty from cooking and carrying.'

'The whole family has dirty hands!' said the first boy, and all three of them tittered together. 'So You're not to come near us or touch us at all!'

Jesus was very, very angry at what they said about Mary and Joseph. He kicked their marbles and sent them rolling all over the street. 'I don't want to play with your marbles!' he said. 'I've got better toys than those! I've got toys *you* can't play with!'

'You've got nothing!' said the rich boys. 'Go away!'

And Jesus went away. He went to his mother, Mary, and asked for one of her old spindles. He took it to where the sunbeams were falling in long yellow stripes through the leaves of a fig-tree, and He twisted one of the sunbeams round the spindle, and turned the spindle, and wound the sunbeam on to it. He could do that because He was the son of God.

He went back to the rich boys and said, 'Look at My toy.' Their eyes grew wide and greedy when they saw the brilliant, hot sunbeam wound on the old wooden spindle. 'I can spin thread of sunlight!' Jesus said, and He began to spin the spindle-weight and to draw out a gaudy, glowing, twisting thread of humming sunfire.

'Let me have it!' shouted the first rich boy.

'Oh no,' said Jesus. 'It's Mine. My mother gave me the spindle and she wouldn't want Me to let you play with it.'

'My father will buy it for me!' said the second boy.

'My father gave Me the thread for nothing, and nobody can buy it,' Jesus said.

'Oh give it us, give it us, let us have a turn!' cried all the rich boys.

'No, no, you can't have a turn at this,' Jesus said; 'but I know another game we can play, and you can have a turn at that.'

'Oh, what is it, what is it?' they asked, all crowding round Jesus and forgetting what their mothers had told them about playing with the carpenter's son.

'It's this!' Jesus cried and, flicking the spindle, He sent the sunbeam thread flying from it into the air. It flew, dazzling, high, and then fell towards the ground in a curve like a rainbow. There it stayed, a shining golden bridge. 'Let's play "Runing Over the Bridge"!' Jesus shouted, and He ran on to the sunbeam bridge, and up and up . . . The three rich boys squinted and shaded their eyes, and squinted until the tears ran as they tried to see Him against the glaring, blazing sunbeam bridge. Standing at the very peak of the bridge, in the sky, with fire under His feet, Jesus waved and shouted to them, 'Come up here! Climb the sunbeam!'

And the three rich boys did. With shouts and squeals they ran on to the bridge, on to its fire – and it bore them and it didn't burn them. But while they were running up the bridge, Jesus was running down the other side, to the earth again.

He turned and saw the three rich boys at the height of the bridge's curve – and then Jesus broke the sunbeam. Down the three rich boys fell, out of the sky, to smack the earth. They were all killed.

And Jesus laughed, because He had His revenge for what they had said about His father and mother, and He had paid them back for their selfishness. He threw the broken sunbeam away and went off to play with His real friends.

The three rich mothers sat at home waiting for their sons – well, they had nothing else to do. They waited until it got dark, but the boys didn't come. So out they went to look for them.

They met each other, and they all said, 'Oh, I thought my boy was with you – !' Then they were even more worried and went into the village. They asked the village children if they had seen their sons (even though the village children were dirty and common). 'Oh,' said the village children. 'Jesus killed your sons because they wouldn't let Him play marbles. He left their bodies over there in the field.' You can never count on your friends not to tell on you, not even when you're the son of God.

The rich mothers went to the field, and they found the bodies of their dead children. They picked them up and carried them to Mary's house. 'Mary, come out and see what your Jesus has done,' they said. 'Come out, Mary, come out and see.'

Mary came out, drying her hands. When she saw the three dead children and the three sobbing mothers, she was sorry; but when she heard it was Jesus' doing, she was furious. She went back into the house, and fetched Jesus out by the ear. 'Now, Young Man,' she said, 'You just put right what You've put wrong.'

'But, Mother, they said you had dirty hands!' Jesus squealed.

'I don't care what they said or didn't say, You just do as I tell You.'

'But they said Father had dirty hands! They said their mothers said you had dirty hands!'

The faces of the rich mothers were red. They all began to explain to Mary that when they'd said she had dirty hands, they hadn't meant it to sound like *that*.

'Never mind,' Mary said. 'He'll put things right if

He knows what's good for Him.'

Despite the pain in His ear, Jesus managed to say, 'Rise, and walk.' The three dead boys got up, alive again, and went home with their mothers – who were so pleased that they forgot to say 'thank you' to Mary.

So it was a happy ending for the rich, as it usually is, but not for Jesus. Mary took Him inside, laid Him across her knee, and flogged Him with a bunch of long, whippy withies – branches cut from a willow tree. She flogged Him till she was exhausted. Then she said, 'I've beaten You to teach You that even if You are the son of God, You mustn't do as You like without thinking of other people. You mustn't kill people just because You can; and You mustn't hurt them just because they're stupid snobs and hurt *Your* feelings. Remember: they have feelings too, however much You dislike them. You must forgive them, because they don't know any better.'

'How many times do I have to forgive them before I can have My own back?' Jesus asked, through His snivels. 'Five times? Six? Seven?'

'If they hurt You seven times seven times, You must forgive them,' Mary said. 'Or I shall beat You seven times seven times. Now stop that noise, and get from under my feet, and *behave*.'

Jesus went out to the willow-tree. That tree had grown the whippy branches Mary had beaten him with. Many branches had been cut from it, and its top was a round knob – it was a pollarded willow. 'May you rot for giving the branches that hurt Me,'

Jesus whispered to it – He whispered so that Mary wouldn't hear Him. 'And may all like you rot, ever after.'

And ever since that time pollarded willows have been the first trees to rot at the heart. They are always hollow and split, because of Jesus' curse.

It takes time and patience to learn a lesson. Who knows how many more times Mary beat Him before He learned it?

This story is based on the traditional ballad *The Bitter Withy*, which gives an unexpectedly ferocious view of Christ as a child. *The Curse on the Willow* is a kindlier version, bringing the dead children back to life.

The Bitter Withy

As it fell out on a Holy Day,
    The drops of rain did fall, did fall,
Our Saviour asked leave of His mother Mary
    If He might go play at ball.

'To play at ball, my own dear Son,
    It's time You was going or gone,
But be sure let me hear no complaint of You,
    At night when You do come home.'

It was upling scorn and downling scorn,
    Oh, there He met three jolly jerdins;*
Oh, there He asked the jolly jerdins
    If they would go play at ball.
*boys

'Oh, we are lords' and ladies' sons,
    Born in bower or in hall,
And You are some poor maid's child
    Born'd in an ox's stall.'

'If you are lords' and ladies' sons,
    Born'd in bower or in hall,
Then at the last I'll make it appear
    That I am above you all.'

Our Saviour built a bridge with the beams of the sun,
    And over it He gone, He gone He.
And after followed the three jolly jerdins,
    And drownded they were all three.

It was upling scorn and downling scorn,
    The mothers of them did whoop and call,
Crying out, 'Mary mild, call home your Child,
    For ours are drownded all.'

Mary mild, Mary mild, called home her Child,
    And laid our Saviour across her knee,
And with a whole handful of bitter withy
    She gave him slashes three.

Then He says to His mother, 'Oh! the withy, oh! the
                                              withy,
    The bitter withy that causes me to smart, to smart,
Oh! the withy, it shall be the very first tree
    That perishes at the heart.'

The Horn

I visited a school and met a boy named Jason, who told me this story.

He said he took some friends from the town to visit a cousin of his who lived in the country. He thought they were going to have a great day, but one of his friends spoilt things by bringing along an older boy named Millfield, who was a real bighead, a right show-off. All the time they were on the bus he kept on about the fights he'd been in, and how much beer he could drink, and all these lies. He had a swastika tattooed on his forehead. He was a proper berk, Jason said.

Jason's cousin Sarah was waiting for them at the bus-stop. She wasn't pleased about Millfield being with them; he was the kind of person who made himself disliked in two minutes. But she didn't say anything because she thought he was one of Jason's friends.

Jason and Sarah took the others round, showing them the river, and the trees they could climb, and the sandstone cliffs and caves, the woods and all the things they'd come to see. Millfield kept trailing after them saying things like, 'Is this the best there is round here? Ain't you got any pubs, or anything good?' Jason wanted to tell Millfield to clear off, but

37

he didn't, in case Millfield was really as tough as he kept saying he was.

One of the other boys, Adrian, was mad about natural history, and animals, and he got on well with Sarah. When they were in the wood, Sarah started telling him that there'd once been this huge forest there, that had grown right over the Midlands and up into Yorkshire, and this little wood was all there was left of it. But there'd been wolves, and deer, and bears in the forest once, right where they were standing. They were getting proper excited, these two, going on about the wolves and bears, so, of course, Millfield had to come up and start: 'How could a wood go from here to Yorkshire? And there's no bears in England. You're stupid.' And when Sarah said there had been, once, Millfield said, 'Well, so what? Who cares? All these trees are stupid anyway. You should cut 'em all down and build some place you can get a drink.'

Sarah turned her back on him, and asked Adrian if he'd like to see some nestlings; and he said yes, so they went off. The others followed, and Millfield trailed after them, deliberately making a lot of noise, to frighten away any animals that they might see. Jason turned round and saw that Millfield was pulling branches off the trees, breaking saplings in two and just doing damage, for no reason. 'Stop that,' Jason said.

'You going to make me?' Millfield said. Jason had *known* he would say that.

Jason told him that he shouldn't tear the trees,

because they were alive. 'They're about as alive as you are,' Millfield said. 'Anyway, if I want to break 'em, I shall, and there's nothing you can do to stop me.' So Jason ignored him, since arguing was only making him worse.

The part of the wood Sarah took them to was quite a way. Every few yards there would be a great rush of birds into the air, and bird-cries all about them, and then a deep silence stretching away through the trees, a silence that seemed to echo with the sound of wings. Sarah said the birds were wood-pigeons, and their being disturbed like that meant that no other people had been there for a long while, and by flying up the birds had warned all the animals in the wood to keep quiet and still.

'The old days must have been like this,' Adrian said. 'Isn't it great?' There was nothing to tell them that it was the twentieth century except their own clothes, and it was so quiet. It could have been Roman times, when there were bears, or the Middle Ages, when there were wolves – they might have gone back in time without noticing it. It was a bit frightening, but really great, Jason said. They thought that, any minute, a bear might come along through the trees – but instead, Millfield came clumping along, saying how stupid everything was. He'd have frightened off any bears that might be about. 'You're the stupid thing,' Jason said to him, and Millfield said, 'I'll put one on you in a minute. You want to take me on? I'll kill you.'

He always got you into conversations like that. He was so boring.

'Oh, *shut up*,' Sarah said, and he did. Sarah brought them to where the nestlings were, and they took it in turns to peer into the nest from a distance at the ugly little things, all opening their beaks. They were careful not to get too close, or touch, because Adrian said the parent birds wouldn't come back and feed the little birds if they did; and Sarah said that was right. Then somebody spotted a squirrel, and they turned to watch that. When they looked at the nest again, Millfield was standing there. And he'd taken the nestlings from the nest, and broken their necks, and dropped them on the ground. He stood grinning at them, sort of proud and ashamed at the same time.

They stood and stared at him. Now why had he done a thing like that? What good had it done him? He made you feel sick and tired, Jason said.

Sarah said, 'You'll be sorry you did that.'

'Who's going to make me sorry?' he said. 'You going to get your Dad on to me? I'll kill him. I've got a knife, you know.' And he pulled this knife out of his pocket. He thought he was so tough.

'Let's go,' Sarah said, and walked away, and the others went with her. Millfield followed, shouting that they were scared, scared, scared, and big babies. They didn't answer him back, because the sound of his shouts among the trees was frightening – not because they were scared of *him* so much, but because it was as if no one should shout like that there – like you shouldn't shout in a church and you feel bad if you do. Millfield's big, yobbish yells echoed from the trees, and travelled a long way, and you got this creepy feeling that *something* – something a long way off – might hear and come. But Millfield went on yelling, because he thought he was annoying them.

The way Sarah was taking them went deeper into the wood, and the paths were more over-grown. It was hard to get through, a lot of the time. Millfield was making a smashing, crashing row, breaking his way through the branches. They came to a little stream, where the ground was black mud. A big tree was growing there, and hanging on the tree was a bow and arrows, and a horn, a real, old-fashioned horn, for blowing, like you see in films. The arrows were in a long bag, made of leather – they could tell by the smell that it was leather – and the arrows smelt of wood and feathers. The bow was hanging by its wooden part from the bag of arrows, and it was a long bow, longer than any of them were tall – except for Millfield, maybe.

They stopped and looked at these things. The stream made a tiny, trickling sound as it ran beside them, but it was dead quiet there. They were scared to speak, or even to make a noise by moving. And they were scared to touch the things, they were so strange. Not the sort of things you expect to find, even in a forest, these days. Who had put them there?

41

Then Millfield came up and said, 'Somebody's been playing Robin Hood!' And he started shouting, 'Come out, come out, wherever you are! Come out and let's see you in your little tights and your little green hat!' His voice went off for miles through the trees, and kept coming back in echoes. The others heard little, quick rustles of movement in the leaves around them, and then the quiet would be even quieter, until Millfield started bellowing again. If there was somebody about – somebody who'd left that bow and arrows there – then that person could hear Millfield all right, and knew exactly where Millfield and the people with him were – but *they* couldn't hear or see the owner of the bow and arrows.

They told Millfield to be quiet, but that only made him worse. 'Tell you what,' he said, and he was unhooking the horn from the tree. 'Robin Hood's supposed to come if you blow his horn, isn't he? Shall I blow it and see if he does?'

'Robin Hood blows his horn to call his men,' Sarah said. 'And you'd better leave it alone. You don't know who it belongs to. Put it back.'

'I don't care who it belongs to,' Millfield said, and he blew the horn. It made a peculiar noise, a bit like a trumpet does when it's blown by someone who doesn't know how to play it properly. But he blew it again, two or three times.

Sarah suddenly started running away from the tree, and they all ran with her – except Millfield. They didn't know why. But as soon as Sarah moved, it was as if she pulled them with her on a string.

You know that feeling you get when you're on your own in the house and you're *positive* that there's somebody standing right behind you, watching you, Jason said. It felt like that after the horn was blown, but it was even more scaring, because it was in a forest, not a house. It was as if every tree was alive, just as he'd told Millfield, but alive and staring too. The silence in the forest – which was full of little noises and breaths – got quieter and quieter, but even more full of little noises and movements that you couldn't quite hear or place, but which were all around, on every side. It was as if a net had been put round that place in the forest and was being pulled tighter and tighter, as something came nearer and nearer.

Behind them, they could hear Millfield laughing and calling them names, and tooting on the horn, just as if he hadn't noticed anything – but then they heard him give a yell. They didn't see what had happened to him, because they were facing the other way and running. But Millfield started running himself. They knew, because of the noise he made. And he was yelling at the top of his voice. He sounded really scared, but they couldn't tell what he was saying.

They were out of breath, and they stopped running and listened. All they could hear for a while was Millfield – but then there was another sound. They all recognized what the sound was, but it was a long time before they would admit it, because it was so frightening. A long time after Jason and Sarah told each other what they had thought at the time, and they both agreed that the sound had been the sound that an arrow makes in films and on television. The sound of an arrow being shot from a bow, flying fast through the air, and then hitting something. But since neither of them had ever heard an arrow being shot except on television, they couldn't be sure that was what it was. But after that sound, they didn't hear anything of Millfield.

They were afraid to go looking for him. They all ran home to Sarah's house, and they told Sarah's Mum that they'd lost a friend they'd had with them – they didn't say anything about the horn, or the bow and arrows, or what they'd heard. They were too scared.

Millfield hadn't turned up by the time the boys went home, and he didn't show up at his own home either. So he was reported missing, and people started looking for him. He was found, in the wood, close by where he'd killed the nestlings. He was lying face down in the leaf-mould, with his arms spread out, and he was dead. There was nothing to show why he'd died, and there certainly wasn't an arrow in him. Jason read the report in the newspaper, and listened to it on the television and radio, and none of them said anything about horns, or bows and arrows, or even of there having been anybody near Millfield when he'd died. 'Local boy found dead in wood' – that was all. There had to be an inquest, and the Coroner said he'd died of heart-failure. But he'd only been seventeen. 'So it was weird, wasn't it?' Jason said.

I asked Jason if everything he'd told me was true. He said it was, and he knew it was, because he'd been there.

'It's a good story,' I said. 'Your cousin Sarah was right – there was a forest, hundreds of years ago, that went from the Midlands up into Yorkshire. Know what it was called?'

'Yeah,' Jason said. 'Sarah told me. It was Sherwood Forest. So like I say, it's weird, isn't it?'

To Dine With the Devil

This is a true story because I say so.

It's about a Vicar who loved to eat and drink. He got out of bed looking forward to his breakfast; he spent the morning dreaming about his dinner, the afternoons dreaming about his tea, and the evenings trying to think of excuses for taking another bite or sip. Nothing pleased him more than to be brought a present he could swallow, be it brandy or strawberries, bacon or cream.

Everyone in his parish knew about his love of food, but word of it had spread much further than that. One morning the Vicar picked up an invitation from his doormat: 'His Infernal Majesty, Lucifer, Prince of The Seven Hells, cordially invites you to dine with him on Friday. The Infernal Carriage will call for you at twelve midnight.'

The Vicar was alarmed, but could not stop thinking of all the wicked luxuries, the sinfully rare and extravagant delicacies, that must be found on the Devil's dining-table. 'Just one meal with the Devil,' he thought, 'and then, for all my life after, I could be good. What's a meal, after all? What could it hurt?' And he decided to accept the invitation.

He knew that it looked bad, though, to keep company with the Devil. So he went to the blacksmith and asked him to make a long spoon. 'A long-handled spoon,' he said. 'One that'll keep a distance between me and those I eat with.'

The blacksmith made him one with a handle as long as his forearm. 'Much longer,' said the Vicar, 'much longer.'

So the blacksmith made him one as long as his arm. 'No, no – much longer still,' said the Vicar.

The blacksmith made the longest spoon ever seen, a spoon as long as the Vicar was tall. 'That's the one!' said the Vicar.

On Friday night there came a Hellishly loud knocking at the Vicar's door. Shouldering his long spoon, he opened it, and there stood a carriage, so dark that it couldn't have been seen, except for the glowing scarlet of its silk lining where the door stood open. The Vicar got himself and his spoon inside, and away the carriage went. It went so fast that it had reached its destination before it had moved. The Vicar climbed out to find himself in Hell.

Among the fires and the cauldrons stood a long table, covered with dishes and plates of the richest, rarest and most succulent foods, just as the Vicar had hoped and dreamed there might be. At the far, far end of the table, almost out of sight, sat the Devil. At the other end, a place was set for the Vicar.

'Please take your seat, sir,' the Devil called. 'The soup is ready and hot.'

Though the table was so long, his seat was still

closer to the Devil than he wanted to be, and the Vicar dragged his chair further away.

'What is the matter?' asked the Devil.

'I don't like to be too close to the table,' said the Vicar. He seated himself, and measured the distance to the table with his long spoon. Waiting imps thought he was ready, and came forward to begin serving the soup. But the Vicar was not yet far enough away. He was still close enough to the table for it to be said that he was in the Devil's company. 'And people judge a man by the company he keeps,' he thought. So he got up again and dragged his chair still further away.

'Is something wrong with your chair, sir? Will you have another?' the Devil asked.

'No, no,' said the Vicar, as he measured the distance with his long spoon. He still wasn't satisfied. He upped and dragged his chair back another few feet, and tried again, and this time his long spoon just reached the table. He was satisfied. 'Now no one can say that I've eaten at the Devil's table,' he thought.

The soup was served. Carefully the Vicar extended his spoon to his dish. The spoon was hard to manage. He dipped it in the soup and, hand over hand, brought the bowl of the spoon back towards his watering mouth. He touched it to his lips, and it was hot, but it was also the most delicious, savoury, salty, meaty flavour he had ever tasted.

The Devil, at the other, distant, end of the table,

moved. As easily as he might have picked up the wine-glass in front of him, or snapped his fingers, Lucifer seized the Vicar by the scruff of his neck. With an easy flick of the arm, he tossed the Vicar over his shoulder into an bubbling cauldron, where he sank and disappeared.

The Devil sighed, and finished his soup. 'Whoever touches one sip or crumb of mine, *is* mine,' said the Devil, and called for the next course.

At the end of his meal, his imps brought him the long spoon, which the Vicar had dropped. The Devil thought it a pretty trinket and hung it on his watch-chain. 'A long spoon?' he said. 'You need a long, long spoon to dine with me!'

Mrs Sugar

I know this is a true story, because when my Aunt Peg was a little girl she used to live next door to Mrs Sugar, who was a witch. Mrs Sugar used to curl her hair with rags and take snuff, and every Saturday she had a bet on the horses. Everybody in the street knew she was a witch. She used to give you silverweed for freckles and camomile for belly-ache.

Anyway, Mrs Sugar died, and she was buried in the cemetery, and had an angel on her grave. Soon after a story started going round that Mrs Sugar was still taking her usual walk out on Saturday evenings. I don't know how the story got started. Maybe people thought that since she'd been a witch when alive, she'd be a ghost once she was dead.

Most adults said the story was just a story, but most children believed it, and they used to go in gangs to the cemetery, especially on a Saturday night, and peer through the railings, trying to spot Mrs Sugar coming out. If a cat stuck its leg in the air, they all raced off, screaming that they'd seen something move. A lot of them *said* they'd seen Mrs Sugar, but none of them really had, and nobody believed them.

After weeks of this game, they got bored with Mrs Sugar, since she never turned up, no matter how long they watched for her. In fact, when my Aunt Peg got the idea to scare her friends, she'd forgotten all about Mrs Sugar. It was Hallowe'en coming up that gave her the idea – they'd had lessons at school about ghosts, witches and Hallowe'en. The teachers said that ghosts looked like people with bedsheets over their heads, and that witches all had cats and flew about on broomsticks. They never said anything about snuff, silverweed and horse-racing. So Peg never gave Mrs Sugar a thought.

What Peg did was to take a bedsheet from home and sneak off with it. That wasn't hard, because her mother worked at night, and Peg could do as she liked. She and all her friends used to run the streets till all hours, and she knew that her friends would come looking for her. They'd search the glass-tip, the marl-hole, the brickyard, and they'd go up and down the canal towpath, looking under the bridges. She only had to hide at one of these places and wait, and they would all come along sooner or later. Then she'd jump out and scare them to death!

The towpath was nearest, so she went there, and she crouched down under the hedge, amongst all the long grasses and bushes. She pulled the sheet half over her head, to be ready to jump out, and she waited.

She knew that it was going to seem like forever,

waiting for her friends, because the time you spend waiting always seems longer than it really is. So she was patient, and even when she was fed up she stuck it out. She didn't realize how dark it was getting, because she was by the canal, and it's always lighter by water than it is anywhere else. Then she heard someone come through the bushes behind her – 'Oh damn!' she thought: her friends had found *her*. She turned round, but the sheet flopped over her face and she couldn't see anything but white.

Whoever it was stood close beside her in the grass, and said, 'Hello, Peggie.'

Peg pulled the sheet away from her face, and saw an old black skirt, thick, white wool stockings, and a pair of battered old button-up boots. The voice above her said, 'You're here to frighten, Peggie?'

Peg looked up, and saw Mrs Sugar.

Mrs Sugar bent down and looked close into Peg's face. 'And I'm here to frighten – let's frighten *together*!'

It was a week before Peg's heart slowed down. Nobody would believe her when she told them she'd seen Mrs Sugar. 'That old story,' they said.

I believed her, when she told me, when she was my Auntie Peg. 'Don't believe books,' she told me. 'Them teachers get stuff out of books. But witches don't have pointed hats, and ghosts don't look like sheets. I know they don't, because I saw Mrs Sugar.'

The Bull

I've been to the church where all this happened, and there was a plaque on the wall, telling the story, and a carving of the bull in its snuffbox. So it must be true. They wouldn't put such things in a church if it wasn't true, would they?

It happened a thousand years ago, when Christianity was a new idea. The village didn't have a church or a priest to keep the Devil away, and the Devil was strong in that neighbourhood. He used to rush up and down the village streets in the shape of a giant bull, frightening people, and, at night, he would follow them along dark lanes in the shape of a haystack – and only somebody who's been followed home late at night by a haystack knows how frightening that is.

Eventually the villagers got together and built themselves a church, but they still didn't have a priest. They had to ask the priest from the next village to come and preach their sermons, but he was old, and he drank too much. His own villagers used to call him Boozebelly. And they said he got on too well with his housekeeper. He wasn't the sort of priest you wanted to preach in a new church, and, anyway, he never turned up when he said he would, because of his old bones – he said.

Because he was drunk again, everybody else said.

The villagers begged the bishop for a priest of their own and, eventually, he gave them one; a new, young priest straight out of priest school. The villagers didn't expect much of him, but he surprised them by being an excellent priest, learned and dutiful. They began to make up rude rhymes about boozy villages with boozy priests, and to boast about their own Father. The sin of pride . . .

The Devil had not minded the new church. It was only another building. But he didn't like it when the new priest arrived. He hated the sound of services being conducted; he hated to see women bringing flowers to the church, and the priest going out to visit his flock. The Devil determined to drive the priest away and to destroy the church.

The bull began by changing its shape and scoring the door of the church from lintel to ground with deep clawmarks. It prowled the churchyard at night, snorting, and alarming everyone who came near. It danced on the church roof during Sunday Mass, startling the people from their devotions, and it came rushing in among them as they stood in the church, roaring and stamping and knocking the altar-table down. There was such uproar that priest and people all ran from the church, and listened to the bull's racketing from the yard. Some people thought they were being attacked by Vikings, and ran into the woods to hide.

When the church was quiet, the young priest

went up to the door and peered in. The bull had gone. It had gone because its work of smashing altar and pulpit, statues and chalice, of tearing hangings and ripping vestments, was finished. The villagers were shocked when they saw the rags and splinters the bull had left. The church had cost them a great deal of work to build and furnish. 'It's time we settled this bull's hash,' they said. 'Father: what you have to do is read the bull down.'

Their young priest didn't know what they meant. So the elder of the village sat the young priest down on the churchyard wall, and explained. 'What you have to do, next time the bull comes into the church, is to read the Bible at it.'

'It won't stay for that,' said the young priest.

'Yes, it will. It'll have to. The longer you read, the more it'll have to stay, and the reading will make it go down.'

'Go down where?' asked the priest.

'It'll make it smaller, Father, that's what we mean. And when it's small enough, we can shut it up in a little box, or a bottle, and then it won't be able to smash your church up any more, will it, eh?'

'Will this work?' the young priest asked, because he'd learned nothing about it at school.

''Course it'll work. You'll see – that old devil enjoyed itself so much today that I'll lay ten to one it'll be back next Sunday for another go. Who'll take ten to one?'

But nobody would bet against a certainty; and

the next Sunday, as soon as the service began, the door of the church was crashed down, and in came the bull, sweeping its horns at the people, bellowing and trampling. 'Read, Father, read!' shouted the elder.

The young priest threw open his big Bible, and read the first words he saw – in Latin. The bull stopped in its rampaging, and turned, and looked at him. The elder climbed into the pulpit and took the priest's arm. 'Keep reading,' he said, and the priest kept reading.

The bull came and stood in front of the pulpit and looked at the priest in an unfriendly manner. It began to roar and bellow again when it found it couldn't move its feet. 'Don't take any notice: keep reading,' said the elder. The young priest gulped, nodded and read.

Most priests could manage four hours of talking nonstop in those days, but this was a young, new priest, who hadn't had much practice, and after two and a half hours, his voice was rough and cracked. Every time he stopped for even a moment, the elder nudged him and said, 'Keep reading!'

'But it's not getting any smaller,' the priest whispered.

'It is,' said the elder. 'It's smaller than it was. Keep reading!'

The priest put his head down, and started reading again. He stared at the page until the letters wavered, and he read until his throat was hot, and his voice worn down to a thin, harsh whisper. He had been reading aloud from the early morning to the middle of the afternoon. When he felt himself dizzy, he raised his head – and couldn't see the bull, until he looked at the floor, where sat a little, grumbling bull, the size of a terrier dog. Beyond the bull, the church was crowded with people who had come to watch the shrinking, and had brought bread and beer to keep them going. A jug of beer was handed up into the pulpit. 'Wet your whistle, then get back to it,' said the elder. 'You can't stop now. You've made him angry.'

The priest took a drink, and whispered, 'I can't read any more.'

'Nobody else can read,' the elder said. 'You've got to, lad! Look! He's getting bigger again!'

The priest focused his tired eyes on the bull, and saw that it was now the size of a calf. 'Does it grow again if I stop reading?'

'That's why you've got to keep reading, Father,' said the elder.

So the young priest took another drink, and read. He read the afternoon away, and when his voice dried, he took a drink of beer to restore it and went on reading. By the early evening, he couldn't be heard unless you were in the pulpit with him, and he was tipsy and couldn't turn the pages, or find the line he wanted. By the time the light began to fade, he couldn't see the words, or remember them, or make even the faintest croak. They gave him more beer, to finish the job, and then carried him off to bed. The bull remained in the church, where he had been fixed by The Word. He stayed there all night, with no one to read to him.

The elders woke the young priest early the next morning. 'Father, get up. The bull needs dealing with.'

With a sore throat and a sore head, the priest followed them to the church – and there found that, during the night, the bull had not only swelled back to its original size, but had grown twice as big. There was scarcely room left for the priest and the elder to get into the church.

'Morning, Priest!' shouted the bull, in a voice that made their heads boom, as the priest climbed into the pulpit. 'Read me down, if you can! If you can't, well – I grow stronger.'

The young priest began all over again, at a task that was bigger than before. It was hopeless. His voice had been worn out the day before; it was hoarse and ragged when he began reading on the second day, and though the bull slowly shrank, the priest could hardly force a peep from his sore, swollen throat by noon – and the bull had only shrunk back to its original size. In another hour, the priest could make no sound whatever. His neck bulged as he yelled – but no sound left his mouth. He had read himself dumb. And the bull began growing again. The people – and the priest – sat and watched it, until there was too little room in the church for them. Then they went outside and sat on the churchyard wall and watched. The bull grew so big that its nose poked out of the window on one side of the church, and its tail hung out of the porch. Its horns soon came crashing through the roof, and the very stones of the walls began to groan and twitch. 'Soon, we won't have a church, and you won't have a living, Father,' said the elder.

The priest had nothing to say. He couldn't speak.

Then, tramping along the road into the village, came two people, an old man and an old woman. The old man was dressed like a priest, but it was hard to believe he *was* a priest, he was so grubby and unshaven, so red-nosed and red-eyed. The old woman was fat and out of breath, and dressed in shabby, baggy old clothes, but at least she was clean.

'Save us all!' said the elder, when he saw the old couple. 'It's Father Boozebelly and his housekeeper. How are you feeling today, Father?' he called out. 'How are your old bones?'

'God is not mocked!' said the old man. 'I heard you had trouble, and I see you have. Your church is going to be a heap in another hour,' he said to the young priest.

'He can't answer you,' the elder said. 'He's read his voice away. He's as dumb as this wall.'

'It's a good job we heard and came,' said the old woman. 'Father,' she said to the old priest, 'you start reading, and I'll take the young Father here, and see what I can do for his poor voice.'

It was impossible to get into the church, but the Old Father had brought his own Bible with him, and he carried it up the churchyard path to the porch, and started reading. 'Fetch me some booze,' he said at the end of the first verse, and, 'Make it strong,' at the end of the second. As the young priest went away with the old housekeeper, Father Boozebelly was tearing into Genesis at full bellow, in a voice that sounded like somebody heavy being dragged along a gravel path. He could be heard at the end of the street.

When the young priest and the housekeeper returned to the church – the young priest with an onion in an old sock tied round his neck – they found the bull already shrinking. They sat on the churchyard wall, with the rest of the village, and listened for eight solid hours, as the old priest read and read and read, and hardly seemed to tire. He was used to reading six-hour sermons every Sunday, and a little extra effort did him no harm. When it got dark, they brought lanterns, and by midnight they were able to go back into the church – though the bull still filled most of it – and light the candles in there. And a while after midnight, the old priest cried, 'I've had enough!'

This was what they'd all been dreading. Now the bull would start to grow again, and would grow bigger than it had ever been! But up got the old housekeeper and climbed into the pulpit, and she started reading. This astonished everybody, because only priests were supposed to be able to read, and women are never priests. But the old woman had been Father Boozebelly's housekeeper for a long time, and could read, and read Latin too. She had also had plenty of practice in using her voice, and managed to read for six hours. That took them to the dawn of the next day, and the bull was considerably shrunken: it was only as big as an ordinary bull now.

The old priest got up again, at grey five in the morning, and he read until golden four in the afternoon, which was a personal record of eleven hours of ear-battering. His voice was so rough and harsh all the time that it was impossible to tell whether he was tiring or not, until he called a halt himself. The bull was now the size of a large terrier dog, and it didn't have much to say for itself.

'Let me try now,' said the young priest in a hoarse whisper – his voice had recovered a little. So they let him read, but he barely managed an hour before his voice had withered away again, and the bull was shouting, 'Speak up if you're going to speak!' The young priest climbed down, and the old housekeeper climbed up. The bull was hardly smaller than when the young priest had taken over.

The old lady read until midnight, and she read the bull down to the size of a mouse. The old priest took a dented snuffbox from his vestments, shook out the snuff – everyone nearby started sneezing – and gave the empty box to the young priest. 'Go and put the bull inside that, lad,' he said.

So the young priest went over and picked up the little, mouse-sized bull, put it inside the snuffbox and set the snuffbox on the floor. The lid of the snuffbox wouldn't close, but that didn't matter.

The old priest had climbed back to the pulpit, and was reading again. Now that the bull was so small, it quickly shrank away. In the couple of hours that followed, the people watched the snuffbox lid sink lower, and lower, as the bull under it got smaller and smaller – until the lid was barely open a crack.

'Devil,' said the old priest, 'I'm going to lay you now. You'll be in that snuffbox for a thousand years. Where do you want to be laid, Devil?'

Everyone fell quiet to hear the answer and, from inside the snuffbox came a loud voice, a roar. It said, 'Anywhere, anywhere – but not in the duckpond! Anywhere but the duckpond! Please, please, don't put me in the duckpond!'

'Devil,' said the old priest sternly, 'I shall send you to the Red Sea.'

'Yes, yes!' roared the bull, from inside the snuffbox. 'The Red Sea, anywhere! But not the duckpond!'

The young priest had climbed up into the pulpit with the old priest, and he whispered, 'Won't it be a better punishment to throw him in the duckpond? It would serve him right!'

'You think so, do you lad?' asked the old priest. 'And that's just what it wants you to think. It knows it can get out of the duckpond. It'd be back here to wreck your church within a week. But you can't fool me, Devil,' he shouted. 'Straight to the

Red Sea you go, and there you stay until your thousand years are up!'

Shrieks of rage came from inside the snuffbox, but were silenced as the snuffbox fell shut. The villagers covered it with pitch, to seal it, and they entrusted it to a merchant who carried it to the shores of the Red Sea and threw it in.

So the village church was saved from destruction – but the thousand years is almost over, and any-day now the bull will be coming back from the Red Sea, furious at its thousand-year confinement – so the Vicar had better watch out.

But what I wonder is: what was it that the villagers really shut the bull in? It couldn't have been a snuffbox because, a thousand years ago, there was no snuff in England. Yet there's the picture, in the church, of the bull sitting in the snuffbox, just before the lid drops shut. So it must be true.

Feeding the Dog

This story's supposed to be true.

It's about a witch, one of the really bad kind, a man named Downing.

He'd spent years learning witchcraft, travelling all over the country, to meet other witches and be taught by them. He married a witch's daughter, and they had a horde of children. They kept a pack of cats too, who went out to steal for them, bringing back meat and fish from other people's tables. There were just as many children as there were cats, and some people said that the children *were* the cats; and the only people who doubted this were the people who thought that the children were worse than the cats. Downing and his wife cared just as much for all of them, and anybody who raised hand or stone against either children or cats had to spend the next few days in bed, aching all over, cursed by Witch Downing. And everybody knew that Witch Downing could do worse than make you ache. So, mostly, the little Downings, human and feline, got away with their thieving.

But a farmer named Hollis heard noises in his yard one night, and came out to find three of Downing's children tormenting the pigs in his sty, by hitting them with sticks. He shouted at them and told them to go away, and they threw stones at him, and shouted names. Hollis was so angry then that he forgot about Witch Downing. The children were so used to getting away with everything that they didn't try to run away. Hollis laid hold of the eldest and gave him the first hiding he'd ever had in his life. The other two ran away when they saw what was happening to their brother. They ran home and told their father.

Witch Downing went to see Farmer Hollis the next day, and demanded money in compensation for the terrible injuries inflicted on his poor boy. Farmer Hollis was afraid of what he had done, but he wouldn't back down now, and he said, 'What terrible injuries? I've done him no more harm than I've done my own sons – I've only given him the sore backside that he should have had a long time ago from you if you'd been any kind of a father! What favour do you think you're doing him, letting him grow up thinking he can do whatever he pleases?'

'Don't preach at me!' Witch Downing said. He went home, thinking that no curse he'd ever set on anybody before was bad enough for Hollis.

So he made a thing. He killed a couple of his cats, and he caught a big dog, and he killed that too. He used poisons, and some of the worst magic he'd learned, and he made this thing that he called a dog – it looked something like a dog. But it was so black that you couldn't really see it, and its eyes shone all the time like a real dog's eyes do when light catches them – shone red, or green, and sometimes blue. It was big. At midnight Downing said to it, 'Hollis.' The thing went out, and it didn't come back that night. The next day Farmer Hollis was missing from his bed, and couldn't be found anywhere.

Witch Downing boasted that he knew what had happened to Hollis, and that people had better watch out! No one knew what he meant.

That night, Downing woke up and saw two bright green candleflames floating beside his bed. There was a shape around them, a blackness. Then the candleflames burned red, and teeth showed beneath them. It was the thing, the dog, come back. It sat beside Witch Downing's bed and looked at him. When he asked what it wanted, it made no movement or sound, but waited. When Downing tried to leave his bed, it growled, and he lay back quickly. He spoke incantations for dismissing spirits, but it stayed. At last he said, 'Farmer Hollis's wife.' Then the thing rose and went out.

People began to disappear. Farmer Hollis had vanished, and then his wife had disappeared the night after. The following day the Vicar couldn't be found; and then a market woman vanished. On the fifth night, the disappearance was of a woman who'd chased the witch's cats away with pepper, and on the sixth night, Farmer Hollis's little son.

But Downing no longer boasted. Now he slunk

about and jumped if a dog barked.

People who had nothing much to stay for began to leave the town, and Downing began to run out of names. Night after night the thing came, sat beside his bed, and waited. It was very patient. It waited and waited as Downing, all in a sweat, tried to think of a name he hadn't given it before. Sometimes he kept it waiting almost until morning, and the closer morning came, the more excited the thing was. It panted like a real dog, and stirred where it sat. Downing didn't want to find out what would happen if he kept the thing until morning, and he would gabble out, 'The boy who serves at the greengrocer's!' or 'The girl in the green skirt that I pass in the lane!' And the thing would rise and go out.

Then came a night when Downing, worn out as he was, must have dozed. He woke with a great shock, and saw that the sky was turning pink! And the thing was pacing up and down by his bed, whining with excitement. 'My wife!' Downing cried – and the thing leapt over him and on to his wife. There was a dreadful noise. Downing jumped from the bed and ran away. There was not an eyelash left of his wife when he returned.

But the thing came to his bedside that night; and he could think of no one. When the thing began to wave its tail, he said, 'The baby.' And there was no baby in its cot when Downing got up.

'My eldest son,' he said, the next night; and on nights after that, 'My eldest daughter – Billy –

Anne – Mary . . . And when the last of his children had gone, the thing still came, sat beside him, fixed its eyes on him, and waited.

Downing had nothing to say. Towards dawn, the silence was filled with the drumming of the thing's tail on the floorboards, and a whine from its throat. The light increased – the thing couldn't stay any longer, and its master hadn't fed it. So it ate its master before it left – and who knows where it went, or where it is now?

For all Downing's learning, he had never learned that you can't dine with the Devil without becoming the meal.

The Headmaster's Wife

A teacher told me this story, so I don't know if it's true or not. His name was John.

John said it had happened to him in his first teaching job. The school was a great school to work at, he said. All the children were well behaved: they never, ever, stepped out of line. The cleaners kept the place spotless. And the teachers kept the staffroom neat, even the sink and the teacups were clean, which is unheard of. And the reason for all this was that everyone – children, staff, caretaker, cleaners – were all terrified of the Headmaster. If any of them saw the Head coming, they used to flinch and look guilty, even if they had no reason to. John couldn't understand it. The Headmaster was always polite and friendly to him, and seemed a nice man. He couldn't understand why everyone was so scared of him.

Anyway, soon after John started work at this school, the Headmaster invited him to dinner at his home, saying that he usually invited new members of staff over, to get to know them better. Well, John wasn't all that keen to go, but he didn't want to offend his new boss, so he accepted. When he told others in the staffroom, they all said, 'Oh, don't go. Make an excuse and get out of it.'

'Why?' he asked.

'You don't want to go to his house,' they said. 'You know, he leads his wife a dog's life. It's terrible, the way he treats her.'

'What does he do?' John asked, but they just kept saying things like, 'I don't know how she puts up with it,' and 'Why doesn't she leave him?' and wouldn't tell him.

John thought they were being daft, and he even began to feel sorry for the Headmaster, having such things said about him behind his back. So, on the night he'd been invited, he really spruced himself up, and went along to the Headmaster's house with a bottle of wine and a bunch of flowers.

The Headmaster's wife wasn't about when the Headmaster let him in, but the Head himself was just as friendly and likeable as ever. He took John inside and opened the wine, and poured John and himself a glass. He told John how pleased he was to have him on his staff, and they were chatting about teacher-training when the Headmaster's wife came in. 'Oh, here's Pat,' the Head said.

John was surprised to see that she was a lot younger than the Head – not much older than he was himself. What surprised him even more was that there was another woman, exactly like her, who walked into the room just behind her. John looked from one to the other, and they were the same woman. He thought she must be Pat's twin sister, and he kept expecting to be introduced to her, but the Head and his wife both behaved as if the other woman wasn't there. They didn't look at her, and the Head walked straight at her as if he couldn't see her. It was when he walked *through* her that John realized she really wasn't there – and yet he could see her clearly. He was the only person in the room who could. He said that he felt his face turn white, and he felt all faint and giddy. He didn't believe in ghosts, but that doesn't help when you see one walking about in front of you. He started to say something about the ghost, but his voice had dried up, and by the time he could speak, he'd decided that he'd better keep quiet about it. He didn't suppose that the Headmaster or his wife believed in ghosts either, and to start yelling that there was one that looked just like Pat, copying every move she made, would only cause a fuss. He thought he'd try to get through the evening without mentioning it. After all, only he could see it, and if it was some sort of illness that he had, it might clear up and go away if he ignored it.

They all helped to bring the meal to the table, and the ghost walked behind Pat everywhere and copied every move precisely. If Pat was spooning vegetables on to a plate, then the ghost mimed spooning vegetables on to a plate. When Pat walked into the kitchen, the ghost followed her, walking in exactly the same way. When Pat seated herself, the ghost, behind her, seated itself too – even though it had no chair. Neither the Head nor Pat noticed a thing. It put John off, though he tried hard to ignore the ghost too. But every time his host or hostess looked at him, he was staring at it, and had to jerk his eyes round to them. And he couldn't follow what was being said, because the ghost was making his heart beat fast and his hands tremble. He dropped his cutlery, and couldn't get his food into his mouth properly. He wasn't being a very good guest.

'Are you all right, John?' Pat asked, leaning towards him. He looked past her to her ghostly double, which leaned forward in the same way, and mouthed the same words.

John saw a chance of getting away. 'Well, no – actually. I don't feel well. I'm sorry – I shouldn't have come.'

'Poor boy! I'll get the car out and run you home,' said the Head.

'No!' John said, staring at the double, which had the same expression of concern as Pat did. 'No. Please. Stay with your wife. I think – I think you should.' And he got up and started for the door.

Of course, they followed him. His behaviour alarmed them. But every time he looked towards them, he saw the ghost behind Pat. He was fighting them to get out of the door. And when he did get out, and looked back, he got the worst fright of the evening. He saw Pat in the doorway and, behind her, the ghost, and for the first time, the ghost did something which Pat didn't. It raised its hand to its throat, as if holding something, and drew its hand across its throat. When he saw that, John just ran. He ran until he was out of breath, and then he caught a bus home.

The next day, the Headmaster didn't come to school. By the afternoon there was a rumour that his wife was very ill. At half past three, John came into the staffroom and was told that the Headmaster's wife had tried to kill herself. John sat down in the nearest chair. 'How?' he said.

'She tried to cut her throat – but the Head managed to save her.'

'Well, he drove her to it.'

'Yes, he led her a dog's life.'

John didn't think there was any point in telling about the double. He didn't understand it himself, and didn't expect that anyone else would.

The Headmaster didn't come back to school for a long while, and the school got grubbier, the children got rowdier, and the coffee cups in the staffroom were filthy. Then the Headmaster came back, because his wife was much better, and he was just as polite and friendly as ever, though he looked sadder. Within a week, the coffee cups were clean, the floors shone, and the children were quiet as mice and good as gold.

John said he left the school because he got sick of hearing people say that the Headmaster was a horrible man who had driven his wife to attempt suicide, when, in fact, the Head was the most likeable man in the school. But when he left he still didn't understand any of it, not the double nor why everyone was so scared of the Head, nor why the Head was so nice to *him* if he really was as bad a

73

character as everyone else said.

I tried to get him to tell me the name of the Headmaster, or the school, or at least the name of the town where the school was, but he wouldn't – except that it was in a big city, a big, busy city.

'Rise and Go'

Now here's a true story. It's about Jack Brownlees, who used to keep the pub called The Wander Inn after his parents retired.

The Wander wasn't like the pubs they build now. It was just a little terrace house, painted cream and brown, with a green door, and frosted, patterned windows put in; and a sign outside. The beer was made in the brewhouse in the back yard. Jack lived over the pub, and when it wasn't open, he would sit on the doorstep and watch people going up and down the street, just as if it was an ordinary house.

It was while he was sitting there that a small boy came up to him with a white enamelled jug. 'Can I have some beer in this jug?' the boy asked.

'I'm shut, son,' Jack said.

'That don't matter,' said the boy, 'because I haven't any money. But me mother's poorly bad and I want some beer for her. Her loves a drop of beer.'

'Does her, now?' Jack asked. 'And did her tell you to come and say that?'

'No,' said the boy. 'It was my idea. I want to give her the beer as a surprise.'

Jack looked hard at the boy, and then believed

him. 'So long as you're not trying to play me for a fool,' he said. 'Well! Come on in, me son, let's fill your jug.'

He led the boy into the pub, took his jug and went behind the bar where there was half a barrel of Jack's own best home-brewed. He held the jug under the tap and turned it on, and the brown beer poured into the jug. The boy snuffed at the beer's scent.

The jug was slow to fill. After a few minutes, Jack turned the tap further, and the beer ran faster.

Five minutes later Jack was losing his patience. He peered into the jug, and the bottom was hardly wet. 'Is this a trick jug?'

'It's me mother's favourite jug off the dresser,' the boy said. He had come round to watch the beer pour.

'It's her favourite jug for fetching beer in, I'll bet,' Jack said. He turned off the tap and examined the jug. It was an ordinary, little, pint jug, enamelled white, with a black edge to the rim and a black handle. But Jack knew he'd put a quart into it already. 'Ah well,' he said. 'I promised you I'd fill it, so fill it I will.' And he turned the tap on again.

The barrel ran out long before the jug was half-full.

'What's the game?' Jack said to the boy.

'There's no game, Mister. I just want a sup of beer for me mother.'

'A sup! I don't understand this, but . . .' And Jack led the way into the back room where his barrels of beer were stored. He gave the boy the jug to hold while he broached another barrel, and then started pouring beer into the jug again. 'Likes her beer, does her, your Mum?'

When the barrel was empty, the jug was half full. 'I said I'd fill it, and I'll damn well fill it!' Jack said, hammering the tap into a third barrel. And that barrel filled the jug.

'There,' Jack said, handing the jug to the boy. 'Give your mother my best wishes, and tell her not to go lending that jug round.'

The little boy carried the jug to the door. It didn't weigh any more than a full pint jug should. 'Thanks, Mister.'

'That's all right, Flower. But don't come back too often. Not with that jug.'

The little boy never did come back to The Wander.

Jack went on brewing his beer and selling it, until war was declared, and then, like a lot of other poor fools, he fell for the posters saying, 'What did you do in the War, Daddy?' and 'We think you should go!' He joined the army, and was sent to France.

It didn't take him long to decide he'd made a mistake. He and his mates had a lot to put up with, what with the cold and the rain and the mud; with the bad food and the sergeants, the rats and the corpses. And then there were the people who were trying to kill them.

There came the day when Jack sat down in a foxhole, up to his waist in water, and yelled at the sky, 'Why am I here? I don't want to be here! I'd like to be anywhere else?'

There was a splash beside him and, when he looked, there was the little boy who had brought the jug to be filled, bobbing about in the cold water of the foxhole, looking no older, no bigger, than he had on that day. Jack was too surprised to speak for a while; and then the only thing he could think of to say was, 'How's your mother?'

'She's well, and always thinks of you kindly, and now she's sent me to repay your favour,' said the boy. 'Where do you want to go? Let's not stay around here.'

'Home!' said Jack. 'No! Not home – they'd say I was deserting . . . Oh, anywhere but here!' Shells passed overhead.

The boy took off his hat, waved it in the air and shouted, 'Rise and go, rise and go!' And the foxhole was empty, except for the water washing about and slapping its sides.

When the army couldn't account for Jack, he was declared lost in action – which was a sorrow to his parents. But it was a sorrow to make their happiness greater; for a year after the War ended, in 1919, Jack came home. He came wandering in from the back yard of the Wander Inn one day, dressed in his uniform – but a clean, mended, ironed uniform.

'Where have you *been*, Jack?' his parents asked him, and years later, people were still asking him, 'Where had you *been*, Jack?' No one ever heard Jack give a good answer. He would sit quiet, and his face would change its expression a dozen times, as if he was trying hard to fit his thoughts to words, but after ten or fifteen minutes of silence, all he could ever say was, 'There's no telling . . . no telling. But it was a fair exchange for a jug of beer, a very fair exchange.'